Monika Gutmann

More Fun with Clicker Training

How communication and signing can improve learning with your dog

CADMOS

Copyright © 2010 by Cadmos Verlag GmbH, Schwarzenbek
Copyright of this edition © 2010 by Cadmos Books, Great Britain
Translated by Andrea Höfling
Title Photograph: JB Tierfoto
Layout: Ravenstein + Partner, Verden
Photographs: JP Tiefoto
Editorial: Sabine Poppe, Christopher Long, Dr Sarah Binns
Printed by: Westermann Druck, Germany

British Library Cataloguing in Publication Data
A catalogue record of this book is available from the British Library.

Printed in Germany

ISBN 978-3-86127-983-9

Contents

Introduction – dog training, the next generation

When I started doing clicker training, I was not aware to what extent this would affect my future life. In the year 2000 I held my first clicker in my hand and began to discover a whole new world in a way I had not expected.

Our mixed-breed Rottweiler, Dino, has been able to learn in a way free from violence that it is better to follow his human than to run after a deer. Previous training efforts involving a prong collar did not impress him greatly. My epiphany came nearly ten years ago when our beloved Dino carried me piggy-back across the exercise yard of our dog-training school. People were shouting helpful comments, such as 'You have to throw him on to his back!' How was I supposed to do that when the dog was carrying me on his back? I thought: 'If you're not able to dominate your dog physically (and this applies to the majority of people who own larger dogs), there must be other ways to control them.' While looking for alternatives I discovered the clicker and with it a window for increasing my knowledge and gaining a better understanding of the relationship between human and dog.

Working with a clicker enables two totally different species to reach a common understanding. At last the human can express their approval at the right time, and the dog knows instantly that they have done something right.

We no longer have to wait for our dog to do something 'wrong' – we keep our eyes open for what they do right instead! By doing things in this way the relationship between human and dog, and their lives together, assumes an entirely new quality. Removal of the constant pressure of having to pretend to be the pack leader is a relief for the human as well as for the dog.

Clicker training is no free ticket to a lack of discipline, as is often alleged. I believe that dogs who have trained with a marker know their limits much more clearly, are able to make sense of environmental signals, and have learned to deal with them – always on the assumption that the human is actually giving the dog the chance to learn. Of course we do have rules, because every kind of family life requires a certain number of rules. However, these are not rigid constructs such as 'The human eats first', or 'The dog must always walk behind the human'.

Our dogs have learned our house rules through clear communication. With a marker word I can let my dog know at any time that I approve of him, for example if he leaves the sofa upon my signal, or, conversely, that he is allowed on the sofa in order to get a cuddle. Whenever one of our dogs has a problem, we work specifically on this particular behaviour. None of my dogs has ever defended resources such as food or toys, for instance. I put 'undesirable' behaviour under signal control right from the outset. When a specific signal is given, our dogs leave the sofa, wait at the door, or lie down while we eat. They have learned this without the use of harsh words or 'corrective intervention'. I have every hope that after reading this book you will be able to experience similar success and positive results.

Living together means communication – clicker training means communication

Living with dogs makes our lives richer and more fulfilled. I wouldn't want to live without them. However, in everyday life you will soon encounter problems with communication. The human tries to make the dog stop pulling on the leash or respond to their own name by verbal means, or by pushing, pulling, shoving and coaxing.

We need a common language

The word 'communication' stems from the Latin *'communicare'*. *Communicare means to share, communicate, participate; act together, unite*. A more modern meaning of 'communication' is 'exchange of information'. Nevertheless the original meaning is still preserved. Communication always involves mutual participation and only works if you share the same platform or consensus.

How do dogs share information among themselves? They use body language and scent/pheromones. They don't give each other names, don't teach each other 'Sit' and 'Down' in response to a signal, they don't call each other back from pursuing a fleeing hare. When dogs are dealing with each other (doing something together – communicating), it usually relates to social issues: getting food and other resources, closeness and distance, mating. Dogs exchange information via looks, pheromones and body language. Pheromones, for example, indicate whether a female dog is on heat; a look warns of a potential adversary. Communication among dogs is clear, unambiguous and is understood globally by all dogs.

Communication with another species that is moving on two legs and talking a different language, as well as constantly touching everything and uttering all sorts of sounds, is bound to lead to misunderstanding. The flow of information is usually a one-way street: from human to dog. Humans either don't hear the dog's signals, or interpret them mistakenly as an attack on their authority. This is a result of outdated and antiquated 'knowledge' about dogs, or rather wolves. An image has been created of our four-legged friends that depicts the dog as a 'power crazy bogeyman' in the world of humans. Humans have to be on their guard constantly, otherwise one day the dog may come and subjugate them. Are you laughing yet? In recent years these opinions and myths have been laid to rest by reputable biologists and behavioural researchers, such as David Mech. At last the dog is allowed to be a dog again, as much as this is actually possible in our urban, human-dominated environment.

Dogs use body language to communicate with each other. The posture of the tail and position of the ears are meaningful signals.

'As a good dog owner you have to behave like a dog!'

We humans can't transform ourselves into dogs and behave like dogs. The indisputable fact that we walk the earth on two legs should make this idea absurd. We cannot behave like dogs – it is biologically impossible.

Through domestication – some scientists are even talking about co-evolution – dogs have learned to pay attention to human body language, and to interpret it. Unfortunately we humans often lack understanding of our dogs' signals. This is the reason why the communication between the two culturally different 'foreign linguists' so often ends up in a conundrum.

Signals – signs – emotions

The one thing we do have in common, however, is the ability to learn new signals, to recognise them and to give them a meaning. This always involves emotions. We cannot switch off our emotions – they are always involved in the learning process. This prevents us from making the same mistakes over and over, and indicates good as well as bad circumstances. Dogs learn quickly, and without any conscious human effort, what happens when the doorbell rings, or what it means when you reach for the leash. The emotional association when you reach for the leash is joy – the dog is looking forward to the anticipated activity, a lovely walk.

Conversely a signal can announce something unpleasant, or cause anxiety. In order to see the dog display signs of anxiety it's often enough to walk in the vicinity of the vet's surgery, or to its entrance. The dog trembles, salivates and refuses to walk any further. Many creatures have the ability to recognise signs and to react accordingly, and conversely to send out signs, i.e. to be the protagonist.

For the communication between human and dog to be successful, we first have to create a basis for an exchange of information (communication) to take place. Dogs don't understand the content of our words. They merely hear sounds that we repeat again and again during our lives with them, and they register the way we express them: loud, menacing or nice and friendly. Dogs have to learn the behaviours that are necessary for the human environment. They are influenced and limited in their natural development by the use of leash and harness. That's why sharing a common basis for communication, i.e. a common language, gives you an advantage that provides security. In our case the common language is represented by the clicker or the marker word. These signals are clear – as clear and unambiguous as the communication among similar beings – and they also influence the emotional position of the other partner.

When the clicker and marker word have been learned, they are able to tell the dog reliably when they have done something right, and that they are going to get something important from their human for their efforts. The human is able to tell their dog, without ambiguity, what exactly the dog has done correctly. It works with great precision, and this form of communication reaches the dog as clearly, and to the point, as it was meant: 'Well done! This warrants a really good reward!' The pleasant side effect of this is that the marker signal (clicker/marker word) evokes positive emotions, just as reaching for the leash reliably triggers positive anticipation.

During my work with the clicker I have often heard it said, and have also read, that the 'advantage' of the clicker relies on the fact that it is 'neutral', and that the dog is getting a 'value-free' piece of information. This always makes me wonder where the human aspect is supposed to be found in this statement. The human being is always the decisive element with respect to training the dog – with or without the marker. The human will always betray their emotions through their facial expression and body language.

Neither does the supposedly 'neutral' information lack emotional content on the part of the dog, because the click evokes feelings of positive anticipation of the promised reward, giving the motivation to continue working on a task. The click comes from a human, and not from a food dispenser. In addition, clicker training doesn't happen in the absence of language.

Of course I talk to my dog during training, I stroke him, and I'm pleased when something works out well. After all, my physical presence is a form of communication too! The information content of the common language between human and dog is clearly emotional. The click is the signpost telling the dog to carry on (joy, motivation); no click is an indication (frustration) that the displayed behaviour is not what I had been expecting from my dog. As a human being I can't hide my facial expressions in this situation. Working with markers is very emotional and it does affect the emotions.

I would like to quote the communication scientist Paul Watzlawick: **'You cannot not communicate – you cannot not behave. Communication functions when both communication partners are in agreement about the aspects of content and relationship.'**

This is clicker training precisely! The human, as well as the dog, has a clear idea what the click means: 'Well done – carry on the good work – you can collect your reward from your human.' Communication could not possibly be any clearer!

Things were a lot better in the old days!
But was it really better in the past? 'In the old days you never used to need any of this new-fangled stuff!' On a positive note, it has to be said that until about a hundred years ago dogs were still allowed to give off a warning in a dog-like manner in our part of the world. Children were admonished not to taunt or tease a dog. If the dog thought it a nuisance to have its ears pulled, and subsequently started growling or snapping, it was considered to be perfectly within its rights. In most cases the pushy child would probably have been punished for upsetting the dog. However, among the negative aspects of the 'good old days' were the prevailing training methods. They had nothing to do with conscious learning, but consisted only of mechanical obedience training. Dogs who turned against their 'masters' by defending themselves did not get to live very long. Nowadays dogs have to live in a world in which they are not allowed to growl, or to have enough space for exercise. Dogs are required to be friendly, peaceful, beautiful and nice. They are not allowed to be afraid, and aggression has been banned from their behavioural repertoire altogether.

Just bear one thing in mind: Dogs have never had the option to choose their family, or to walk away if they don't like them. Dogs are forced to live with 'that' human being. Aren't these reasons enough to make you decide in favour of animal-friendly training methods? We owe it to our dogs to prepare them for an environment in which typical canine behaviour and aggression are to a large degree no longer considered acceptable. Therefore it seems paradoxical to want to cure aggression with the use of aggression on the part of the human – biology, behavioural science and neurobiology have provided us with many arguments to support the theory that aggression cannot be tackled with the use of aggression. For this reason, if we want to modify behaviour or emotions, we need training techniques that are adapted to our current level of knowledge – and clicker training is the logical consequence of studies in the aforementioned disciplines.

Living together means cooperation – cooperation is good for all involved

What is cooperation?

Cooperation suggests two or more living beings acting in combination with each other, which typically leads to a mutual advantage. The lives of humans with their dogs should be characterised by cooperation.

Individuals of some canine species cooperate with each other if there is a potential advantage that one individual can't achieve on their own, for example providing food by hunting large game. In addition, life in a group provides security. Cooperation even occurs between different species (symbiosis) – a well-known example is the clown fish and the anemone. The fish is protected from the stinging nettle cells that are very unpleasant to other marine creatures by a mucous layer. It 'dwells' inside the anemone where it raises its brood in safety. In return it defends 'its' anemone from predators.

Cooperation means evolution – together you can achieve goals that would be unattainable for one individual alone.

Cooperation can't be forced, at least not for joint acts from which everyone involved benefits to the same degree. Forced cooperation leads to one of the participants always emerging as the winner. In the best case scenario for a forced community this cooperation doesn't do too much damage to the other partner. Cooperation is based on communal activity.

Cooperation means communication

Cooperation can only work if there is communication on an equal footing. The clicker/marker signal provides the basis on which communication between human and dog can take place. Clicker and marker signals are an offer to cooperate. This cooperation has a positive outcome for both parties involved in the agreement. The human experiences attention and affection from the dog, and the dog gets attention/affection and gratification of their physical needs.

Remember: We cannot not communicate! Through the use of the clicker/marker signal we can, consciously and directly, communicate with the canine foreign language speaker who shares our home, and cooperation takes on a new quality. It is not a one-way street from human to dog, in which we ask something of the dog, but it is also a line of com-

A dog who has learned that cooperating with his human has benefits, and who can be sure that a friendly human is waiting for him – such a dog is happy to come back.

munication from dog to human, through which the dog receives feedback from the human via their innate behavioural patterns. In this way the dog learns social competence, such as tolerance of frustration if the reward doesn't materialise immediately, or isn't meeting expectations. In addition, the dog recognises which desired behaviour will lead to success in their particular environment. The easiest way to achieve this would be by speaking the same language, wouldn't it? When the human trains with the dog, this always means that social interaction is taking place – after all, dogs don't sit in front of a fruit machine gambling for their dinner.

Successful cooperation is characterised by mutual attention, gratification of needs, good communication and a positive exchange.

Cooperation means communication, means attention

A common language is useless unless my communication partner gives me their full attention. With regard to our relationship with dogs this means that our actions are not

Attention coming from both directions is communication!

Sitting together in a street cafe and enjoying the day. Emma has learned to pay attention to Maria even with a high level of distraction.

happening in a human to dog one-way street, but that the dog is learning to divert their attention away from things that are important to them and towards the human instead. Communication and cooperation always involve attention on both sides.

However, the mammalian brain has its quirks. It is unable to process all the huge amount of stimuli and information it is constantly exposed to. As a result it has to be selective about which bits of information are important in a particular situation, and which aren't. *Paying attention is vital!* Those bits of information that are not important for the organism in a particular situation are blotted out. *Attention means turning (orientation) towards a selected object*. To do this, other bits of information are pushed into the background, and they aren't stored in the memory either.

This provides us with the next important component of attention: The selection is made according to the importance of the information.

First to be processed are danger signals and unknowns. Unusual things attract attention, because they may represent danger. In addition, attention tends to turn towards information that is emotionally charged. This is indirectly relevant to the organism, because it provides signals regarding the importance of information. This means that unusual things are evaluated with respect to their significance – a threat of danger, the chance of food, etc. The greater the emotional significance of the information for the individual, the more attention is given to it.

Needs and interests play a decisive part in the emergence and distribution of attention. If a dog is hungry, this need determines to a great extent what sort of thing will attract its attention. A mouse rustling in dry leaves will be given attention, because this signal may mean the potential gratification of a need.

There are a number of basic attributes that will attract attention from all living creatures:

- Size and intensity of stimulus (hot–cold, hungry–sated, sudden loud noise, flash of light)
- Movement (the movements of one object moving away from other objects, approaching objects, etc.)
- Colour (focusing on contrasts, certain colour combinations)
- Contrasts in the environment (objects against the light)
- Clear and regular edges
- Striking symmetry
- If the object is in a particular spot within the field of vision, for example top left.

Emotionally charged information is given attention. The click/marker signal is a very emotional piece of information. This signal indicates the gratification of needs (attention/affection, social interaction, food, etc.) with, or with the help of, the human.

The click is the signal for cooperation, communication and interaction.

How
it all began

The American biologist Karen Pryor was the first to use a marker signal in the training of dolphins in the 1960s. You can't get dolphins to adopt certain behaviours by putting them on a leash, and there's even less of a chance to teach them anything by using punishment. Wild animals react to punishment either by withdrawing their cooperation (refusal of cooperation) or by use of defensive aggression.

How is it possible to establish communication with a marine mammal? The idea was simple as well as ingenious. Pryor linked a whistling signal with food. Every time the signal was sounded, the dolphins got a food reward – fish. During further training only the 'correct' behaviour was marked with a whistling signal, and this became the signal to indicate that the behaviour displayed at that particular moment was correct, and would be rewarded in due course. The whistling sound was not a 'command'!

In the late 1980s Karen Pryor, together with Gary Wilkes, applied this communication system to working with dogs. They were, however, not the first to train dogs with the use of a marker. The biologists Marian and Keller Breland were working with dogs using something resembling a clicker as early as the 1940s. But it was Karen Pryor whose work made this approach for the training of dogs known around the world.

Nowadays this training approach is employed by many zoos in order to prepare animals for veterinary treatments, or to make their daily care more pleasant for all concerned. In this way elephants learn to put their leg on a platform in order to have their pedicure done; with the help of a clicker they experience this treatment as positive. They cooperate willingly with their keeper.

In the two decades since working with a marker signal has been introduced to the world of dogs, much has happened. There was a great deal of further development, many methods were tried and changed. That's the beauty of working with marker signals. The work is varied, communicative, leaves room for finding new solutions and offers ever more challenges to the human–dog team.

What actually is learning?

Working with living creatures (humans as well as dogs) should be based on a good foundation of knowledge. It's not enough to do something and just keep your fingers crossed that it will work out. Knowledge helps us to develop and change things. By reading this book, you are about to expand your knowledge through learning, and perhaps to modify your own behaviour as well.

According to Zimbardo (1992) 'learning can be defined as a process based on experience which leads to relatively stable modifications in behaviour or in the potential of behaviour.'

In the chapter 'Communication' (see page 10 ff.) I have already described that dogs, as well as humans, create an emotional and also a rational association between certain signs and events, and pay varying degrees of attention to them. This is the simplest way to learn something about our environment, as well as the consequences of our actions. In the animal kingdom the warning sounds made by one species also signal danger to other animals; signal colours mark out animals and plants as inedible or dangerous.

It is important to recognise the signs of danger quickly, and not to waste any more energy on investigating it. An animal that keeps ignoring the rattling of a rattlesnake will sooner or later lose its life.

Signals that announce food or the gratification of a need are characterised by recurring irregular rewards. Energy is expended on these, because this safeguards survival. It is vital to recognise these signs and act accordingly.

In the psychology of learning, the learning of a stimulus is called 'classical conditioning'. It was discovered and researched at the beginning of the twentieth century by Ivan P. Pavlov. According to this approach a previously neutral stimulus receives a meaning. As we recognise these stimuli we are able to negotiate our way around our environment, and to act accordingly. Even the learned sign by itself can trigger fear or joy. That's why we get an uneasy feeling when we hear the whirr of a dentist's drill, or we happily remember a recent beach holiday upon hearing the sound of waves. Visual signs, sounds, touches and smells are always connected with the centre of emotions in the brain. Smells in particular reach the part of the brain that is responsible for emotions without any diversion.

This kind of learning is difficult to influence and goes on every minute of our lives. It is important to know what the consequences would be if you were to heed or to ignore a sign. Will this be followed by something good or something bad?

The meaning of the 'click' is learned on exactly this basis: Something really good is associated with a sound (sign).

Summary:
- With signal-based learning (classical conditioning) a stimulus is associated with emotional meaning.
- The signal develops a predictive quality – this gives the individual security and control in their environment.
- No conscious behaviour is learned.

Trial and error – trying out what is worthwhile

With classical conditioning learning is often passive, and this doesn't explain how new behaviours emerge. Learning new things is an active process. The individual displays a spontaneous behaviour, and the consequences of this action decide whether it will be repeated or not. In terms of learning biology this is called *operant* or *instrumental conditioning* – learning by trial and error.

This theory was pioneered by Edward Lee Thorndike, who formulated the *'law of effect'* in 1898: *'If a certain reaction is followed by satisfactory consequences (reward) in a certain situation, the association between the situation (the stimuli present) and the reaction will be affirmed or reinforced. If the organism enters the same or a similar stimulus situation again, the reaction will be displayed with a greater probability than before.'* (Translated from www.wikipedia.de)

To put it more simply: Every positive consequence of a particular behaviour will affirm this behaviour in the individual concerned, and it will be repeated. The consequence has to be perceived as something positive by the individual. It is important to realise that what may be pleasant for one individual may not be considered worth striving for by another.

Thorndike furthermore established the hypothesis that behaviour will be 'reinforced' by satisfactory consequences.

Conversely there is the *'negative law of effect'*: *'If a behaviour in a certain situation is followed by negative (aversive) consequences, the probability of this reaction recurring in that situation will decrease.'* (Translated from www.wikipedia.de)

In addition the learning material will be remembered better through repetition. These basic foundations of learning are the same for every living creature.

A key term used in modern dog training, and in particular clicker/marker training, is *'positive reinforcement'*. This term originates from the research of B. F. Skinner, who investigated animal behaviour in the laboratory but didn't concern himself with the inner processes that an individual undergoes during the act of learning. For Skinner learning was a mental process that is a no-brainer as far as animals are concerned; instead he used the word *'conditioning'*.

'Conditioning' describes the learning of a stimulus–reaction pattern without taking into account inner processes such as emotions and thoughts.

Influencing behaviour –
the conscious use of consequences

Behaviour is displayed more frequently if the resulting consequences are satisfactory for the individual in question.

Behaviour will be displayed less, or not at all any more, if it is answered in a negative or aversive way (refusal). Take a look at the 'square of consequences' (see picture).

In this context 'positive' and 'negative' don't represent the evaluation 'good' or 'bad'. Here we're dealing with the mathematical terms of adding (+ = positive) and subtracting (– = negative).

A brief example: We're practising 'Sit' with our dog.

- *Positive reinforcement* = The dog's bottom touches the ground and the dog gets a tasty treat.
- *Positive punishment* = The dog doesn't sit down immediately; he gets a smack on the behind.
- *Negative reinforcement* = Pressure is exerted on the dog's rear end until the dog sits down; then the pressure ceases.
- *Negative punishment* = The dog doesn't sit; you turn away and the treat disappears into your pocket. There are no more rewards.

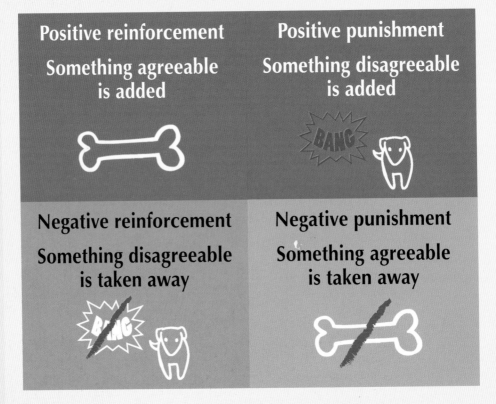

Positive reinforcement
Something agreeable is added

Positive punishment
Something disagreeable is added

Negative reinforcement
Something disagreeable is taken away

Negative punishment
Something agreeable is taken away

Square of consequences.

Dogs are not stimulus–reaction machines. Their behaviour is always linked with emotions, as with all living creatures. In the late 1990s the scientist Jaak Panksepp produced evidence for the existence of an emotional basis for behaviour in animals, and the biologist Mark Beckoff has been researching the emotional lives of animals for decades. Emotions are the key to reliable learning.

'From the viewpoint of the psychology of learning, learning is understood to be a process of relatively stable modifications regarding behaviour, thinking or feeling as a result of experiences or new insights and the understanding (of the processed perception of the environment, or one's own sentiments reaching consciousness).' (Translated from www.wikipedia.de)

We modify the dog's behaviour and emotions through new experiences during training (association). These behavioural modifications become reliable and stable through repetition and practice. As a result of their training our dogs derive an increasing number of 'data' from their experiences regarding how they can act or react in certain situations. The practised signals take on the characteristics of an announcement and affect the emotions. Every signal that has been developed in a positive manner will evoke positive emotions. If a particular behaviour is displayed reliably in many different situations, the dog has learned it successfully. This does not require the use of 'positive punishment'.

Bad behaviour should be punished – or should it?

In terms of learning psychology, the meaning of punishment in the colloquial sense is understood as follows. Aversive stimuli (which are usually linked with a general fear response) are added, with the result that the behaviour is curtailed and will be suppressed in future. The problems with this method of punishment are as follows:

- You have to apply the punishment at the very first instant the 'mistake' occurs.
- The punishment has to be so intense that the probability of the dog committing the same mistake again is reduced almost to zero.
- If you are forced to apply punishment twice in the same or a similar situation, the punishment was either not severe enough, or the dog doesn't perceive the punishment as such.
- In addition you always have to be present for the punishment – the dog will associate the punishment with you.

The use of punishment therefore throws up certain practical problems. You cannot punish a particular behaviour in your absence; the dog will associate negative emotions with you; the dog has learnt that it is safer to do certain things outside your presence or reach.

When using positive punishment the following questions confront the punisher:

- Are you able to apply the punishment immediately, and so severely that your dog will never display this behaviour ever again?
- Are you sure that the dog will associate the punishment with the action perpetrated? If not, the dog will not understand what you have punished them for. There is a huge potential for 'mis'-associations. The best example of this is the electric cattle fence. I know many dogs who have developed a fear of the most improbable things after an unpleasant encounter with an electric fence: a stream, meadows, horses, dirt roads. It is the object to which the dog's attention is directed at that particular moment that will be associated with the sudden pain, and not the wire the dog has touched. Can you be one hundred percent sure of what your dog's attention is directed to at the point of punishment? Pulling hard on the leash upon encountering another dog will have the opposite effect. You are explaining to your barking dog that every time another dog appears, it will have very unpleasant consequences.
- Are you sure that the intensity of your punishment is so well balanced that the dog isn't going to suffer any significant damage from it (physically as well as mentally, for example fear)?
- Are you sure that the dog won't defend itself, and bite out of panic?

As you can see, this type of punishment has to be perfectly adapted to the punished dog, and the situation, in order to be effective in the way it is meant to be. Certain behaviours will be omitted from the dog's repertoire. *With positive punishment no new behaviour is learned, it only leads to the suppression of behaviour.*

How do I tell my dog...?

In the earlier chapter on communication' (see page 10 ff.) I explained what communication is, and how to communicate with your dog in a clear and unambiguous way. A brief word about the background of the marker signal in the biology of learning is now appropriate. The clicker is known as a 'secondary reinforcer'. There are also 'primary reinforcers', which are naturally effective from birth and involve gratification of needs such as food, drink, sleep, shelter, and reproduction.

Secondary reinforcers are learned, usually by linkage with a primary reinforcer. In our human world an example of a secondary reinforcer is money, which we use to meet our basic needs.

If a secondary reinforcer ceases to be followed by a primary reinforcer, its meaning is lost. It becomes ineffective. Therefore a 'click' is always followed by a primary reinforcer.

Thus the 'click' signals to the dog that they have done something correctly, and secondly that something will be coming their way that is important to them. *Behaviour is reinforced through the gratification of needs!* If the signal ('click') is not followed by anything that is meaningful to the dog in this situation, the marked behaviour will not be displayed any more often in the future.

With the clicker/marker signal at their disposal the human has it in their power to

determine what they want to communicate to their dog, and which desired behaviour they want to affirm. Remember: A pleasant consequence for your dog means reward, i.e. gratification of needs.

'The reward system in the brain always produces messengers such as dopamine or the body's own opiate peptides when a behaviour is particularly useful, and this will subsequently be perceived as pleasant.' (Wilhelm, 2009)

Bribery

Again and again I'm told that this sort of thing amounts to bribery, and that my dog only does what he is told because I have a treat for him. He would not do it without the treat.

There is no such thing as bribery in the biology of learning. The term 'bribery' has its basis in the penal code. There it is defined as procuring an advantage by an unlawful act. One party hands out the bribe, the other takes it, in order to act on it. How do you apply this to a dog? In the case I have just described we would expect our dog to take the biscuit first, and then sit down. With a bit of luck he might even do just that. But isn't it rather that, first of all, the dog is told what to do without being handed a biscuit? If he doesn't do it, then the alleged bribe is added. We know that dogs learn by association. They learn to recognise and categorise signs and contexts, and by doing so they are making a statement regarding probable future events. The dog will learn the following

in this context: 'Sit' means that the human will raise a hand with a biscuit in it. If the biscuit in the human's hand is missing, the signal does not have the meaning 'bottom on the ground'. Luring the dog is something you should try to avoid as much as possible. First, because there is a risk of forming an association with the treat/toy. Second, because by luring the dog you prevent them from learning to carry out a task consciously. The dog runs after the treat, and as soon as you have no treat in your hand, they will no longer display the desired behaviour. The proper context is missing, and the conscious body posture has not been retained in the dog's memory. If you want to trigger behaviours, or indicate directions, working with targets is much more suitable (see page 30 ff.).

As far as rewards are concerned, I distinguish between the *structure of an exercise* and, after it has been structured carefully, an *affirmation through variable reinforcement* (see section 'The most important thing: Become variable', page 30 ff.). At the beginning I use a certain number of small, tasty treats for the initial structuring and formation of an exercise, because this enables me to exercise better control over the training units. I also vary the choice of treats – even pizza can become dull in the long run.

During the structuring and generalisation of an exercise a click and reward are always given. Once I have trained (formed) the behaviour in every kind of situation, just as I

Give the rewards in a variable manner, and find out what your dog's preferences are.

had visualised it, I switch to rewards that are adapted to a particular situation and need. You can give your imagination a free rein and try to find out what your dog really likes in certain situations. If your dog likes food, you can use some of the food as a reward when working on the generalisation out of doors. Food can be used in a variable quality and quantity. In addition food gratifies a basic need.

Don't forget that play can also be used as a reward. A toy that you only use outdoors, a food bag, a combination of food and play (throwing morsels of food and letting the dog sniff them out), running games with the dog, letting the dog go for a swim, having them perform a trick.... There are so many possibilities for rewarding your dog appropriately with regard to the situation and their own temperament, and that allow you to do something together at the same time.

If you're expecting your dog to do something with you, you have to show them that joint activities involve a response from you. Just throwing a ball is meaningless, and does not constitute a joint activity. Furthermore you are turning yourself into a ball dealer, and your dog into a ball junkie. Controlled prey-hunting games with a food bag/toy are social activities.

Important!

A reward has to gratify needs. Eating food, for example, is a basic need. 'Bad' treats almost amount to a punishment, and will not motivate the dog, nor will they cause the desired behaviour to be displayed more frequently.

Rewards are dependent on the context; a food reward during a heatwave does not gratify a need. In this situation water and swimming would be the kinds of reward that would reinforce a behaviour. You should increasingly use behaviours that are attractive to the dog as rewards: digging for mice, searching for food, prey-hunting games....

This time Luna doesn't get her reward out of the hand, but she has to sniff out the treat first.

Generalising – 'Sit' applies anywhere

Transferral needs to be learned. Dogs are not good at transferring learned behaviour to other situations. In practical terms this means that you gradually have to associate the exercise with a large number of different environmental stimuli and places. Now you'll say: 'This will take a very long time!' But that's not quite true. The dog has to learn that paying attention to humans is also required in other contexts and other locations.

Most dogs are used to being pushed, pulled or dragged into any required position. If you still have to push your dog into the 'sit' position, then the behaviour has not been learned properly. You can only get your dog's attention if they have a

good emotional connection with you. Dogs who are experienced in training with a clicker usually achieve the transferral of learned behaviour to new situations pretty quickly. It may be helpful to keep a training diary. Write down how often and how long you have practised a new exercise and in what kinds of situation. When you add up the minutes spent, you'll realise that it didn't take that long after all.

If you have structured the exercise carefully, and generalised it, the time has come to reduce the use of clicks and treats.

It is important only to move on to the next step when the behaviour has been perfected and can be called up at most levels of distraction. A half-affirmed behaviour can only be called up half-reliably, because the dog does not understand the point of the exercise clearly. You will be disappointed; you and the dog will end up frustrated, because it just won't work.

The most important thing: Become variable!

Once you have practised an exercise with your dog in many different situations and at various levels of distraction, and you are happy with the execution of the task, you should begin to hand out rewards in a variable manner. Don't give a click and reward after every correct execution of the signal any more. Start doing it at variable intervals: every other 'sit', every five 'sits', then every third time, and so forth. Of course you're allowed to be pleased with the execution of the task!

It is important to vary the rewards for the correct learned behaviour. This ensures that it will

remain stable and can be called up reliably. All animals who hunt first of all have to learn and to perfect their hunting skills. Let's stay with canine predators. Even as puppies or young dogs they practise hunting sequences with their littermates, and apply these gradually to the animated environment, i.e. small prey. Not every hunt is crowned with success. However, because every now and again they will achieve a hunting success, the behaviour stays firmly in place. If you are hunting for mice, and a hare happens to rise up in front of your nose and is

killed, this would be rather a big reward at the end of the day: a great hunting success – a basic need gratified. Even if the dog doesn't catch every hare that they come across, it's enough to be successful every now and again. If a dog never manages to catch a hare, it will cease to hunt hare.

It doesn't make sense for a creature to waste its energy on something that never leads to success, especially where the supply of food is concerned. Food is vital for every creature. Without sufficient food everything stops. Even if our predator doesn't catch hares any more, the hunting behaviour persists. The reward at the end of a hunt can vary. It could be just a little mouse, or occasionally, on the other end of the scale, big game that's been hunted communally. Should our canine predator stumble across a hare and catch it, it will hunt for hare again in the future.

In addition, this example demonstrates that in nature there is not even the smallest hint of a positive punishment in connection with learning and preserving this vital behaviour. If the hunt is unsuccessful, the resulting consequence is an empty stomach. But on their return the 'hunter' is not going to be beaten up by the rest of the family because of their lack of success. Next time hunger strikes, they will go out hunting once more. Maybe this time there will be a deer in the offing!

Tip!

I always carry a few biscuits for my dogs in my pocket. On some walks they don't get a single treat. But I don't want to preclude the chance of a reward if worthy behaviour is displayed by accident. On ninety-nine occasions out of a hundred we don't encounter any game while walking in the forest. But on the one hundredth occasion a deer may jump across my path, and I can successfully recall my dogs. That is worth a jackpot! I also don't see any difference in whether you take a ball with you, or some biscuits. Both can be used for a social interaction with your dog. I like to address my dogs' needs. Both love to search for food in the grass or undergrowth. Only I can make this possible.

Be surprising!

Play around with rewards of any kind. Your dog must not know in advance whether they can expect anything from their human, or what it is. You may say that in this case it is enough, when your dog comes to you, that you are pleased with them. If your dog feels this is worthwhile, then it may suffice. According to my experience, praise and being patted on the head leave many dogs relatively cold.

You would like your dog to display a behaviour more often? Then you will have to find out what really turns them on. Before going for a walk, pack some treats and toys, so on your walk there will be either food, an exciting game, a trick they like to perform, or a digging stint.

Myth: Behaviour will only become reliable if punishment is used during training

Allegedly, a behaviour will only be displayed reliably on demand if it is 'secured' by aversive methods. Let's have a look at training with reference to this allegation. For instance you begin to develop the recall positively. The dog associates positive emotions with coming back to you, and the certain knowledge of what will happen after the signal. The human is pleased; there is play, food and social interaction.

All of a sudden you switch to punishment mode during your training. The new behaviour is punished because of 'disobedience', even though it has not yet been learned correctly. What will happen now? The result will be a feeling of insecurity on the part of the dog, because they can no longer predict what will happen when they return to the human upon the recall signal.

Please bear in mind that signals have the characteristics of an announcement and are always associated with emotions!

In the worst case the dog won't return at all, because they will associate something unpleasant with the recall signal. The dog will prefer to satisfy their needs in the environment instead. There are many variations, for example the dog returns but won't let you put them on a leash, or they move only hesitantly in your direction.

Don't give the dog any room to think that something negative may await them on their return to the human. Develop the signal with

great care and give it a lot of thought. Don't leave your dog in any doubt about how safe and predictable you are for them.

If you give variable rewards you safeguard behaviour – without ever having to resort to punishment. Relationships are founded on security. If you make it a habit always to behave in the same way in a particular situation, you give your dog a sense of security. They can predict what will happen to them.

Myth: Dogs don't treat each other with kid gloves either

Our training group consisted of four dogs: three males and one female. Each time the male dogs weren't 'treating each other with kid gloves', there were resources involved: a bitch on heat, food, toys, human attention. Please observe the context in which dogs are interacting. This has nothing to do with structuring, developing and calling up an exercise!

It would be far better to put your energies into thinking about what your dog does well, and how you can reward them for it. Punishment does not make a behaviour more reliable, and it has too many unpredictable side effects, which will manifest themselves in an insidious way.

Command – signals – vocabulary

Humans are similar in their words, but you can tell them apart by their deeds.

Jean-Baptiste Molière (1622–1673)

Words influence thoughts and deeds. Therefore it is important to get away from the negative term 'command' and to replace it with a positive term. We train our dogs to work with signals: audible or visible signs.

A command expresses the wish for absolute obedience, and, in the case of non-compliance, this leads to the command being pushed through, often with unpleasant consequences for the dog. The dog is forced to do something regardless of the consequences.

It is normal to ignore signs in our environment. Have you never driven through a 20 mph zone too fast, because you were in a rush? You did see the sign with the speed limit, didn't you? But as far as you're concerned you had a good enough reason to ignore the sign. Or have you never stopped in a no-parking zone, because you just wanted to pop into the news-agent's for some sweets or a newspaper? In this case also, the reason why you chose to ignore a signal is of great importance: You just wanted to gratify your need for the sweets or newspaper.

We have the same phenomenon with a 'disobedient' dog. We have to ask ourselves: Did the dog really take in the signal? Was the dog paying attention to us, or were they distracted by the environment to such a degree that they didn't hear us?

You have a dog! A dog evaluates situations differently from a human. If I have structured, developed and generalised a signal properly, the dog knows what it is about, and if they do not carry it out, then there is something wrong. My dog has a problem in this situation. Now I need to engage with my canine partner and try to comprehend the situation in order to help my dog. I increase my training efforts regarding this particular situation.

This is why 'commands' become signals, and these will be called up in different situations. The dog learns them in a similar way to that in which a foreign language student learns vocabulary. If the use of a word in an unfamiliar sentence structure is still a bit shaky, the student needs to intensify their learning.

The structure of the communication signal – Clicker/marker word

In order for the clicker or the marker word to be effective, clear and powerful in any context, you have to structure and develop them in various different situations. The clicker and the marker word are both structured in the same fashion. For the marker word you must choose a word that you don't use in your daily communication with your fellow human beings. You can use an onomatopoeic word such as 'click', 'zack' or 'plopp'. I have two words for our two dogs, one marker word for each dog. The great advantage of this is that I get absolutely clear communication when I go out with both dogs at the same time. For Usha the word is 'prima', and Louis gets a 'goodie'. In households with several dogs, this is a wonderful tool for marking and rewarding the correct dog.

Usha and Louis are being trained using their own individual marker words.

The sequence is relatively simple, all that's required is a little bit of practice. First comes a click, at which point there is no treat in your hand (a). After the click the hand moves to the bowl (b), and then the dog gets the treat (c). Proceed in the same manner with the marker word.

Structuring the clicker/marker word

Prepare two or three bowls with really tasty treats. Each bowl contains about ten to fifteen pieces. Make a click and give your dog a treat straight away. Repeat this until the bowl is empty (click – treat – click – treat ...). Have a brief break (about two to three minutes) and start again. The dog doesn't have to do anything, except to be there and to receive the treat from you after each click. If you are in a peaceful environment and you have your dog's full attention after the click, you can increase the challenge, i.e. the environmental stimulus.

In another exercise unit you develop the marker word exactly like the click. Don't do both at the same time. Remember that the clicker/marker word says to the dog: 'The thing you have done just now was the bee's knees! You have earned a reward from your human.' *The marker word is not praise!* Use the marker word as a way of communicating with as much conscious intent as you would the clicker.

At the beginning do it inside the house in a peaceful environment. Go to different rooms, vary the treats, add more distractions, and every so often change location from time to time. This way you structure and develop your signal for communication, cooperation and good mood step by step, in order to make it work reliably and unambiguously in many different locations and places.

Step 1: Low-level distraction

- Various locations in the house (kitchen, living room, hall, cellar, etc.)
- Vary your position relative to the dog: in front of the dog, next to the dog, etc.
- Vary the reward following the clicker/marker word: different treats, play, or anything else your dog may be fond of.

Does the clicker/marker word trigger feelings of happy anticipation in the dog as well as turning their attention towards the human? Then you can advance to step two.

Step two: Medium-level distraction

- Different locations (garden, quiet street, quiet park)
- Vary your position relative to the dog: in front of the dog, next to the dog, etc.
- Vary the rewards following the clicker/ marker word: different treats, play, or anything else your dog may be fond of.

Does the clicker/marker word trigger feelings of happy anticipation in the dog as well as turning their attention towards the human? Then you can advance to step three.

Step three: High-level distraction

- Different locations (park, street, humans, animals, cars)
- Vary your position in relation to the dog: in front of the dog, next to the dog, etc.
- Vary the rewards following the clicker/ marker word: different treats, play, or anything else your dog may be fond of.

Does the clicker/marker word trigger feelings of happy anticipation in the dog as well as turning their attention towards the human? Then you have done it, and your dog has learned beyond any doubt what the click or the marker word mean in any kind of situation. Now it's time for some goodies from the human!

Overview of the structure for developing the click/marker word: step by step from a low (1) to a medium (2) to a high (3) level of distraction.

Change locations while developing the structure! The clicker is supposed to be a clear and effective sign that is unam-biguous and independent of any context: 'You have done the right thing – a reward from your human is on its way.'

The right order is important. First make a click (see photo page 38), then reach inside the bag and retrieve the reward. The click enables you reach inside the bag and get out the treat in your own time.

In order to achieve an association that is really effective it is important to gratify needs. Dogs who like to use their noses get a reward that needs to be sniffed out after the click – the treat is thrown into the grass.

Vary the rewards while developing the click. The click can also announce a really fun joint play session!

The carry-on and power-up signals

The carry-on-signal is a sign to indicate to the dog that they are on the right track and that they should carry on doing whatever they are doing. At the end of it some goodies will be coming their way in the shape of a marker signal and a reward from the human. Furthermore, this signal is very well suited for explaining to the dog in a friendly fashion that this may take some time, at the vet's for example, when the dog is getting an injection, or having their paw examined, or having someone look into their ear.

The power-up signal is very helpful for the recall. The options for deployment are varied, and here too the possibilities are endless. You can structure this in two different directions: away from the human and towards the human. In the first case the dog can search for food or a toy, in the second variation they follow a movement. This opens up the possibility for great interactions with the human – as a power-up for a reliable recall (see page 44 ff.).

Power-up signals are made up of a long line of short syllables (for example 'tiktiktiktik', 'lalalala' ...). You utter these syllables the whole time while the dog is on the right track, or during the time they are supposed to stay in a particular position. The last syllable is followed by the marker, and then the reward. This positive structure should be freshly 'recharged' every now and again. This way you can use it to modify the dog's mood in unpleasant situations (such as at the vet's). However, if you only ever use the carry-on signal in unpleasant situations, it will become tainted with negative emotions. Negative emotions in unpleasant situations are not what we're trying to achieve with our communication.

The carry-on signal

Lay out some treats in a calm environment. Leave quite large gaps between the treats. Tie the dog up about two metres away. They can watch you as you're laying out the treats. Go to your dog, take the leash and move towards the treats. Keep repeating your signal syllable while you're doing this (1).

Just before reaching the first treat, make a click (2) and your dog takes the morsel of food (3). The dog can walk on the leash ahead of you in the direction of the food; assign a name to this forward motion. As soon as the dog moves towards the next morsel, say your

Overview of the structure of the carry-on signal.

signal syllables again and follow the sequence as demonstrated in the drawing.

As with developing the click/marker word, a thorough transferral to a multitude of situations and environmental stimuli is of vital importance. Increase the distance to the treats, put the favourite toy at the end – use your imagination; the possibilities for variations are endless.

By using the carry-on-signal you can help your dog with many different behaviours, for example staying in the 'sit' position for longer,

Transferral to the wider environment. The bowl contains a few treats. On the way there keep repeating the bridging signal – 'takatakatakataka'.

continuing a search, fetching, walking at heel, walking on the leash – any exercise that requires continual work.

It is possible that the dog will associate only movement and change with this signal, and that they will start getting nervous during calmer exercises. In this case it would be advisable to develop an additional signal for calm behaviour. Have the dog sit, and then show them a treat or a toy.

For as long as the dog is sitting down, a new syllable is sounded for being calm (1). End with a click and the reward, i.e. toy/food (2).

Begin to use variations, to generalise: no toy/treat in your hand, change the dog's position (down, stand up), change your position relative to the dog (in front, behind, next to), increase the distance, put one hand on different parts of your dog's body.

Make a click at this point! The dog is allowed to eat the treats out of the bowl.

Overview of the signal for calm behaviour

The power-up for the recall

This variation is used specifically for the recall. Use a syllable that you can call loudly, in quick succession and in a friendly voice. For my dogs I use 'Yippieyippieyippie' as a power-up signal – this has a wonderfully cheering quality, and it has almost a calming effect on me when my dogs move towards me and away from, for example, a deer. The power-up exercise always ends with some fun activity with the human:

playing with a favourite toy, searching for treats, super-jackpot, food, or whatever else tickles your dog's fancy.

Begin working on the power-up signal for the recall at a short distance; a distance of two metres is sufficient. Call out your power-up signal and move backwards away from the dog while looking towards them (1). As soon as the dog has caught up with you use the marker, and play with your dog. Have an active playing session with your dog close to you (2). If you're not sure that the dog will stay with you, put them on a leash for this.

Overview of the structure of the power-up signal for the recall.

Begin giving the power-up signal at a very close distance – 'yippieyippie!' As soon as your dog has reached you, make a click and begin a nice joint play session. Only when this works well at a close distance should you expand the exercise and start working to improve it.

The power-up signal is the announcement of really good things to be had from the human. While Maya is running towards her owner Maria, she keeps hearing her signal. Once she has reached Maria, she gets a click. This is saying to the dog: 'Well done – here's something really nice for you!'

Maria retrieves the favourite toy from behind her back, and a fantastic tug-of-war game ensues. Doing something together with the human builds and strengthens relationships!

Different types of targets: A children's puzzle piece as ground target, a fly swatter, a pointing stick, a cooking spoon, and a home-made target stick (from left to right).

The target – an aid for guiding, and positioning

Targets are aids used to position the dog, or to trigger a movement that the dog doesn't display spontaneously. A target may be touched with the nose or a paw.

'Touch' – touching the target with the nose

The signal 'Touch' asks the dog to touch a hand or other object with their nose. It is developed as follows. Briefly hold your hand in front of the dog's nose; most dogs will instantly sniff it. With the other hand make a click and give a reward. Use ten to fifteen treats for one

Hold your hand close to the dog. Thomas practises a two-fingered touch. The two extended fingers lend the signal an unambiguous visual quality.

Luna touches the hand with her nose – 'click' and reward.

①

②

Click

exercise unit, then have a break, and then have another exercise unit.

In order to develop the signal, increase the distance between the dog and the hand, and change the angle of your hand relative to the dog (1). If the dog touches the hand reliably, control this with a signal (2). From this point onwards, any voluntary touching of the hand will no longer receive a click.

Once your dog touches the hand only following the signal, the already familiar sequence for transferral and reinforcement of the signal follows: change the location, increase the level of distraction, vary the treats.

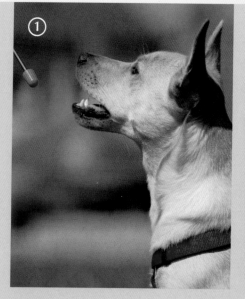

Hold the target stick close to the dog's nose. At the beginning keep it as simple as possible! Maya is unsure about what she is supposed to do with this strange object.

Click! Super! Keep repeating this and and stick to the same structure for exercises as described on page xx 46. to ensure that the target will be touched reliably and in any situation.

Generalise the behaviour in many different locations and situations.

Transferral to other objects

'Touch' can be used universally and does not necessarily have to be confined to touching the hand. For example, transfer the 'touch' to the target stick (see photos 1–3).

The ground target

By working with a ground target, the dog learns to step on to a mat or a particular spot.

Developing the different targets is an enjoyable challenge for dogs and humans alike. Once the target has been learned, you can build many exercises and tricks on it to give the dog mental

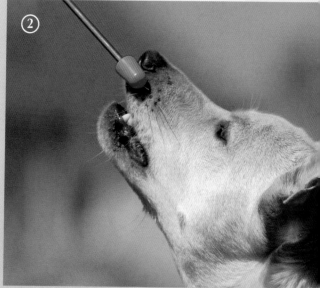

Every time the ground target is approached, or a paw touches it, a click and a reward are given.

As soon as Emma touches the target with her paws – 'click' – and here's a reward from Maria.

exercise. For example, a slalom through the legs with the target stick or hand target, jumping across an outstretched leg, or sending the dog ahead using the ground target.

In this way the dog doesn't have to be lured into certain positions by having them run after a treat. By practising this regularly the dog will learn to use their body more consciously.

The name game – communication and cooperation, reorientation

In order for communication to work without ambiguity, the dog has to learn to associate their name with paying attention to the human. The signal must be clear and positive, in anticipation of things to come.

The sequence of the exercise is very simple (see pictures page 52–53). You throw a treat away from the dog; as soon as they take the treat, you say the dog's name (1). If the dog looks at you, make a click (2) and throw another treat (3) or a really nice toy (4) away from the dog.

If your dog initially has a problem with turning towards you after you have called their name, begin very close to the dog and throw the treat on the ground right in front of them. As soon as the dog has taken the treat from in front of their nose, you say their name. If the dog looks at you, make a click and throw another reward on to the ground in front of them. If that works well, you can begin to throw the treats further away. Begin to change your position relative to the dog. Sit, or stand, in front of the dog, behind, and next to the dog. The name is supposed to represent the reorientation towards the human.

In order for the name to become a really strong reorientation signal for your dog, you have to transfer the signal to many different places and distraction levels. Use a variety of foods (quality and quantity), play activities (toys and the duration of playtime with you), other activities (running, swimming, etc.), and other signals that have been developed in a positive manner ('sit', 'here', 'handshake').

During further training your dog will initially look away when there's a distraction. At this point you only call their name once. If your dog doesn't look towards you because of the distraction, slowly count to ten and then call your dog's name again. With a bigger distraction it may be helpful to take a step sideways should your dog not look at you straight away. Make sure you only call your dog's name. Don't make any coaxing noises! Your dog is supposed to associate their name one hundred percent with their orientation towards the human. Only train with distractions that your dog is able to cope with.

Overview of the structure for the reorientation signal/name game.

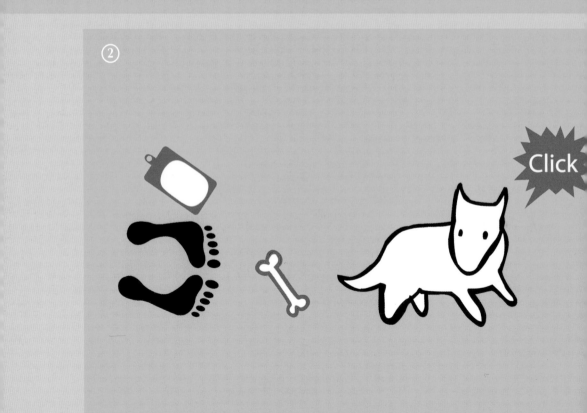

③

④

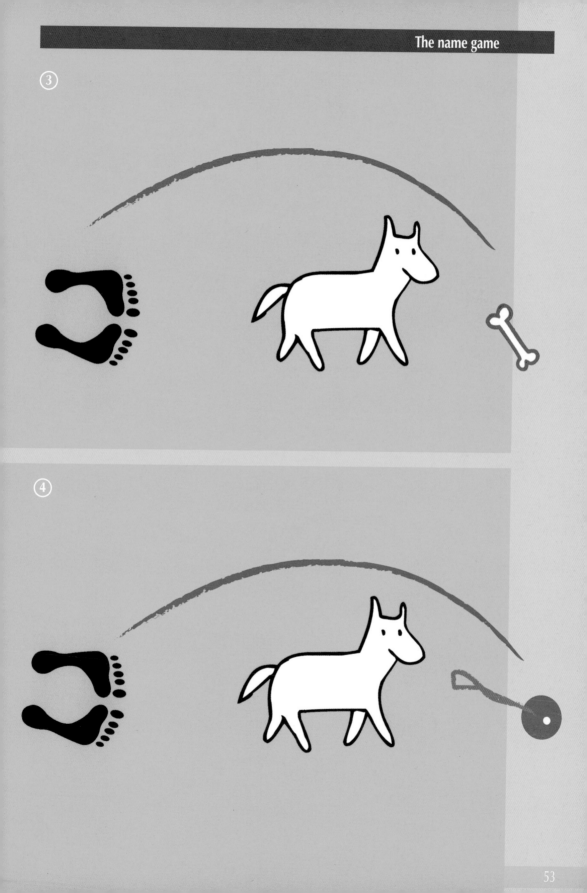

The dog is looking away – call their name.

Emma looks towards Maria – 'click' – Well done! The dog's own name should always mean an orientation towards the human.

If you have trained well with your dog, you can increase the challenge. The name is followed by a positive exercise: 'Emma' – she looks towards the human – 'click' – 'sit' – reward.

Vary your position relative to the dog. Luna is not paying attention. Astrid addresses her.

Luna looks towards her – 'click' – followed by a reward whilst walking.

The goal of an exercise could be, for example, 'Sit'.

The basic structure of an exercise

At the beginning you have to decide what you want from your dog, and what exactly this behaviour is supposed to look like. Then you must split the behaviour into small steps and help your dog, by means of the marker, to find their way around.

Sit

1. What is the dog supposed to do?

When you think about what your dog is supposed to do, describe the desired behaviour/action in every detail and decide what you expect from him. For example: 'Sit' – the dog puts its bottom on the ground and is supposed to leave it there, until they get a different signal. Even an exercise as 'simple' as this has several components!

2. Marking behaviour

Once you have made a conscious decision regarding which behaviour you want, you

have to begin to reinforce each tentative move towards the correct behaviour. Clicker training has the wonderful advantage that you gain the ability to 'read' your dog much better. You recognise changes in muscle tension and body posture which remain unnoticed with classical training.

Start the session in a very peaceful environment in which neither you nor the dog is distracted. *Remember: clicker training means attention!* A dog who has not learned that paying attention to the human is worthwhile will be easily distracted in an attractive environment, and will no longer pay any attention to you.

3. Perfecting behaviour

If your dog performs the movement 'bottom on the ground' reliably inside the house, you can begin to increase the challenge. What kind of 'sit' do you want? An exact 'sit' with both hindlegs parallel, or are you not fussed whether your dog sits on just one cheek every now and again?

Practise in many different locations!

4. Controlling behaviour with a signal – only one word per action/ behaviour!

When you're happy with the behaviour (body posture, speed), you can assign a name to the action: 'Sit' – the dog puts its bottom on the ground – click and reward. From now on you will only make a click after first saying the signal. Voluntary sitting will no longer be rewarded. Once your dog knows what 'Sit' means as part of a calm exercise unit, you have to start to generalise this exercise.

5. Generalising – transferring behaviour

Because dogs find it difficult to transfer behaviour to new situations, you have to modify or increase the number of locations and the amount of distraction slowly. Begin to practise

Practise with distractions.

in other quiet locations. Increasing the distraction usually involves a change of location as well. To be on the safe side, in exciting situations you should give more frequent rewards, depending on the training status.

Important!

If there is a higher level of distraction and excitement, you have to mark and reinforce the correct behaviour sooner and more often. Only proceed to varying the rewards when everything works to your satisfaction, even at a high level of distraction.

6. Become variable

Once you have trained everything carefully and your dog really knows what it's all about, you should begin to *vary* the frequency of the rewards. There doesn't have to be a reward every time! Begin with short intervals, for example every second signal is reinforced with a marker signal and a reward, then every fourth signal, then again every second, then every fifth signal and so on. Vary the reward frequency until you end up having to mark and reward only on rare occasions in order to maintain the signal/behaviour in question. This last step should only be undertaken when the behaviour has been carefully generalised, and you can be sure that it will be performed without fail following the signal.

*...verview of the basic structure of an exercise. Define desired behaviour (1), mark it (2), perfect it (3),
...t it under signal control (4), generalise it (5) and reinforce it in a variable way (6).*

Down – Lie down

The signal whose structure I describe here has nothing to do with the usual 'Down' performed during exams at dog training school. It is a further variation of a calm exercise; in this case the duration of the execution will be varied. Your dog should have mastered the hand target and the bridging signal for this.

Structure: Begin once more in a peaceful environment. Hold your hand as a target slightly below the dog's nose (for execution of the exercise see photos 1–3).

For calm exercises I prefer to use treats that don't excite the dog unnecessarily. I only integrate any play action once my dog is familiar with the exercise.

Your hand target moves onto the ground – pull the hand slightly forward on the ground and wait. Take your time – most dogs work out quickly that they're supposed to lie down.

A great start – the direction is right. Just wait one short moment and let your dog think about it. Do not click yet!

The dog is lying down – click! Now you can pull out the goodie bag or a toy.

Practise in various locations. Even if it looks as though the dog is lured with a treat – he isn't.

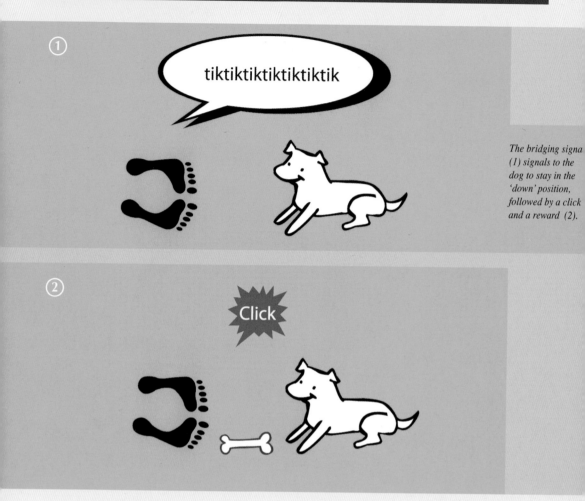

The bridging signal (1) signals to the dog to stay in the 'down' position, followed by a click and a reward (2).

Affirm the exercise as described on page 58 ff. Use increasing levels of distraction and practise in many different locations.

Until now we didn't have an audible signal for lying down. The hand target signals 'Lie down'. In order to get the association with the appropriate verbal signal, proceed as follows: Say 'Down', followed by the hand target – the dog is lying down – click and reward. It is important to be clear about the correct sequence of events: verbal signal, hand target – click and reward. If you are saying the signal and giving the hand target at the same time, your dog will be unable to make the connection that it is the word that contains the meaning 'Lie down'. When you have repeated this exercise many times in this order, finish by saying your verbal signal. As soon as your dog lies down – click and reward! Don't give them any assistance. The signal 'Down' is supposed to replace the hand target.

Now you have 'switched' the signal, you can begin once more to generalise it. Modify your position relative to the dog, change locations and distractions.

In the following sessions you can increase the amount of time during which your dog remains in the 'down' position with the help of your bridging signal.

Begin the training in your home environment – practising walking on a leash also requires attention.

Walking on the leash

It appears that for many dogs the issue of walking on a slack leash is hard to come to grips with. Usually these dogs have learned from puppyhood that pulling on the leash gets them from A to B, i.e. to places where they can have a good sniff. This behaviour is doubly reinforced by the following scenario. As soon as the dog has reached the desired spot by enduring the unpleasant sensation that pulling on the leash causes to their neck, the unpleasant sensation stops. This in itself is a reward (see negative reinforcement, page 24) and now the dog can have a good sniff, which represents another reward (see positive reward, page 24 ff). As a result the dog learns that pulling on the leash is a worthwhile activity.

However, our aim is for the dog to learn that the leash is a signal for 'I will stay within this radius around my master/mistress'. Walking on a slack leash has nothing to do with doing 'heelwork' for an exam.

Marking and perfecting behaviour

The first steps to training 'walking on a slack leash': marking the behaviour (1) and perfecting it (2 and 3).

Step 1: Without a leash or harness

Begin by moving around in a relaxed manner at home in your kitchen/living room. Your dog is without a harness and not on a leash. As soon as the dog begins to follow you around, full of curiosity – click and reward. Give them the reward out of your hand. Every step that your dog takes as they are walking next to you – click and reward. Develop this behaviour further, step by step.

Step 2: With a harness, but without a leash

Begin the same way as in step 1. After the first bowl of treats put the harness on the dog and proceed as in step 1.

Step 3: With the harness and leash

Begin in the same way as in step 2. After the first bowl of treats attach the leash to the harness and proceed as in step 1.

Step 4: Using variable rewards

Use rewards in a variable manner, and only give a click for every second, third, eighth, second or fifth step.

For the execution of each of steps 1 to 4 use three to four bowls of treats.

Generalising behaviour and rewarding it in a variable manner

At home you can add further distractions by practising inside the house when the children are at home, or when friends are visiting. A-gain, you should begin by having only a low level of distraction (e.g. the children are present, but doing their homework) and slowly increase the level of distraction. Then you can transfer your training to the outdoors. Go into the garden and practise steps 1 to 4 out in the open. If you don't have a garden, find a peaceful spot on a lawn or in a car park and practise

Further steps for training 'walking on a slack leash': generalising the behaviour and rewarding it in a variable manner with a treat (1) or a joint play session (2).

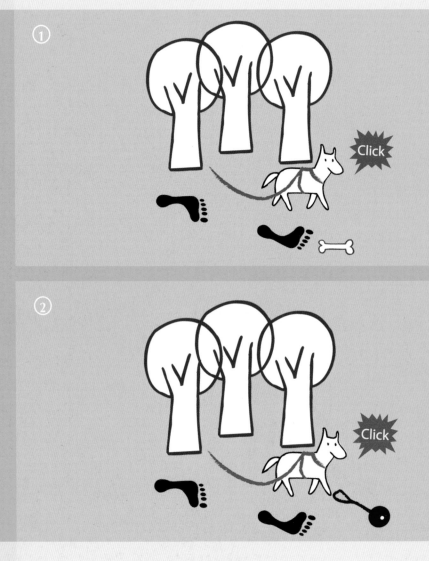

only steps 3 and 4. For this to be successful you have to be absolutely sure that steps 1 to 4 work one hundred percent at home. And don't forget to use the rewards variably.

Tip!

If you are unable to practise during 'normal' walks, and you have been using a collar and leash, then leave it at that, even if your dog is still pulling on the leash. You can make things a bit more comfortable for your dog by switching to a wide padded collar. For your own comfort you can use a retractable leash.

A single step suffices! 'Click' and reward.

Begin by also giving clicks for every step your dog walks next to you on a slack leash while walking outdoors. Include many changes of direction. If that is working well, expand the exercise again. I like to take my cue from objects in my environment. In a car park with marked parking lots the first mini-goal I set myself consists of walking from one white line to the next with a slack leash; once we've reached it I give another click and a reward to the dog. If this doesn't work, I aim for half a parking lot, and give a click and a reward then. This way I don't have to keep counting continually, and I can use objects in my environment for training purposes. When you have managed to cross the whole of the car park with your dog on a slack leash without a single click – congratulations are in order!

The reward is given whilst walking.

Important!

Vary the training. Practise with the clicker on one occasion, and then use a marker word for the next unit. This way the marker word stays fresh in the dog's memory and will be transferred to other behaviours. With the marker word you always carry the tool you need for communicating with your dog with you. Deploy the marker word with the same sense of purpose as the clicker!

If you do your training in the street you can, for example, use the distance from one lamp post to the next lamp post as your point of reference for the clicks. Street lights are usually spaced about twenty metres apart. You can begin by commuting between them. Start next to a lamp post, and at first make one click at every second, fourth, eighth step. If your dog pulls on the leash during one of the stages, change direction and walk back to the starting point with the leash hanging loosely down. If the dog pulls on the leash again on the way back, turn round and walk towards the other street light. In this manner you end up, so to speak, walking from pillar to (lamp) post.

It is important to ensure that your dog will no longer get what they want by pulling on the leash. If you allow your dog an occasional success as a result of pulling on the leash during the training stage, you will achieve your goal (to have the dog walk on a slack leash) only with great difficulty. Please bear in mind that behaviour that has been reinforced in a variable manner will be imprinted on the memory more strongly the less

frequently it is reinforced. This means that, if within two weeks your dog manages just once to reach the nearest tree by pulling on the leash, you have been the instrument of your own downfall. Unconsciously you have signalled to your dog that pulling on the leash is worthwhile, and that they might just as well try it more often.

Tip!

If your dog pulls on the leash with great force, and you are unable to hold them because of the disparity of power, and the dog drags you all over the place as a result, a headcollar, such as a HaltiTM, may give you additional control. One end of the leash is attached to the harness, and the other to the headcollar.

Before you begin training, you must get the dog used to the headcollar. Begin by pulling the headcollar briefly over the dog's nose – click and reward. If your dog starts to stick their head inside the headcollar voluntarily, you can try to close it behind the head – click and reward, and immediately take it off again. Increase the time period during which the headcollar stays on, and once your dog accepts it happily, begin with steps 1 to 4 as mentioned above (see page 65).

The headcollar is used only for better control, not for corrective purposes. Don't tug or jerk on it!

If you are unsure about how to use the headcollar, harness and leash, contact a professional dog trainer (see list at the end of the book).

The leash slackens just a tiny bit. If the dog sits down, that's fine. Make a click and carry on walking immediately.

Problem: The dog still pulls on the leash occasionally

As soon as the dog begins to pull, the leash tightens and your arm is moving forward, just stay rooted to the spot like a tree.

Now it is very important that you wait until your dog starts to act. As soon as the dog reduces the pull on the leash, make a click/marker and move to the front *straight* away.

For you this means: Don't talk to the dog, don't lure them, just wait patiently until your dog starts using their little grey cells! In my experience most dogs don't want a treat after the click during the early stages of training. This makes perfect sense: Your dog wants to move ahead, that is their need at this point, not a biscuit. *Please bear in mind that, in*

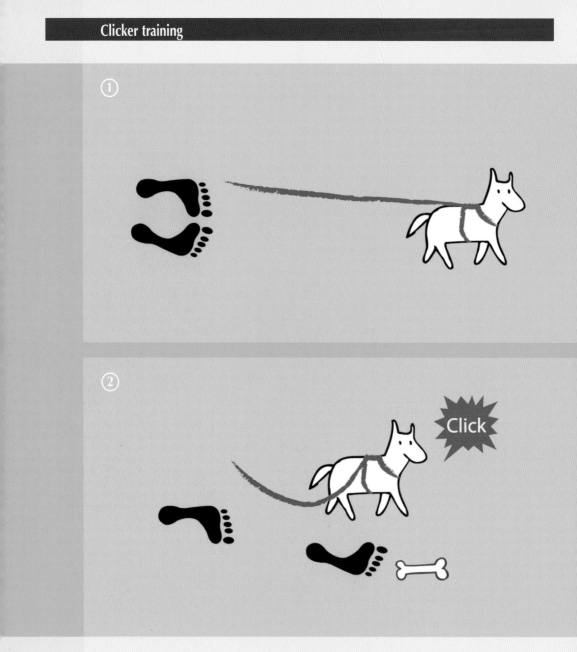

If the dog pulls on the leash, become a tree (1); a click and reward are given only if the leash slackens (2).

order to reinforce behaviour, you have to gratify the dog's needs.

For this type of training it is important to make a click immediately, and to walk towards the dog, as soon as they have taken the pressure off the leash. Don't wait for them to return to you to demand a treat. Give them the biscuit the moment they are next to you as you 'catch up' with them while they are moving ahead.

Important: As soon as the leash tightens – be a tree!

And now for something different – after the click play with your dog!

Tip!

The dog should not return to collect the treat from you after the click, because dogs quickly form 'chains of behaviour' when the chronological sequence of several behaviours happens at short intervals. If you give a click for a slight backwards movement, the dog will come towards you because they want to collect the reward. If you stop walking now, after a few repetitions the following will happen: The dog pulls – they release – click – the dog collects their reward from you – you walk a few steps – the dog pulls – they release – click...
This is an unwanted cycle, and your dog resembles a canine yo-yo. This has nothing whatsoever to do with walking on a slack leash. You must always have an image in your mind's eye of the sort of behaviour on the leash you desire: joint forward movement. Therefore it is important to walk towards the dog immediately after the first click, and then to reward them while they are in the position that you'd like them to be in.

When walking on the leash is working well in a peaceful environment, of course you will also have to transfer this activity to many different locations and levels of distraction – and finally, use variable reinforcement!

It's the dog who sets the agenda. If the dog takes the pressure off the leash – 'click' – start walking immediately and give the reward while walking.

After you have trained conscientiously, there's nothing to stop you from enjoying a relaxed walk through town.

Come back – the recall

One of the most important exercises is training a truly reliable recall. To ensure that the recall will work even with a high level of background distraction, it must consist of three significant building blocks:

1. *Reorientation* – This requires your dog to have learned their name as a reorientation signal (see name game, page 51 ff.)
2. *Power-up* – Your dog has learned the power-up signal (see page 40 ff.)
3. *The gratification of needs* – This may consist of toys, food, food bags, running games, etc.

These three building blocks have to be joined together carefully. First, we begin a short distance away from the dog. A leash two metres long is perfect. The leash is attached to the dog in order to secure them, and to prevent them from helping themselves to rewards in the environment.

In a peaceful environment start by playing the name game once more. A secluded meadow would be good, because we need a bit of space for this.

Once the reorientation with the name game works well, the power-up signal will be deployed. In order to increase the dynamics and the readiness on the part of the dog to follow you, walk backwards away from the dog. When the dog has reached you, make a click, followed by some exciting play with a favourite toy, or food, or something else that is meaningful to your dog.

Once you can manage all three building blocks in the correct sequence, and your dog knows what this is all about, you can begin once more to generalise the signal. In a peaceful environment also begin to increase the distance: Use a longer leash, take off the leash.

Increase the level of distraction only when this works well. Make sure you reduce the distance every time you increase the level of distraction! At first use a two metre leash again. If you have worked on the preparatory training conscientiously, you'll quickly achieve the longer distances once more.

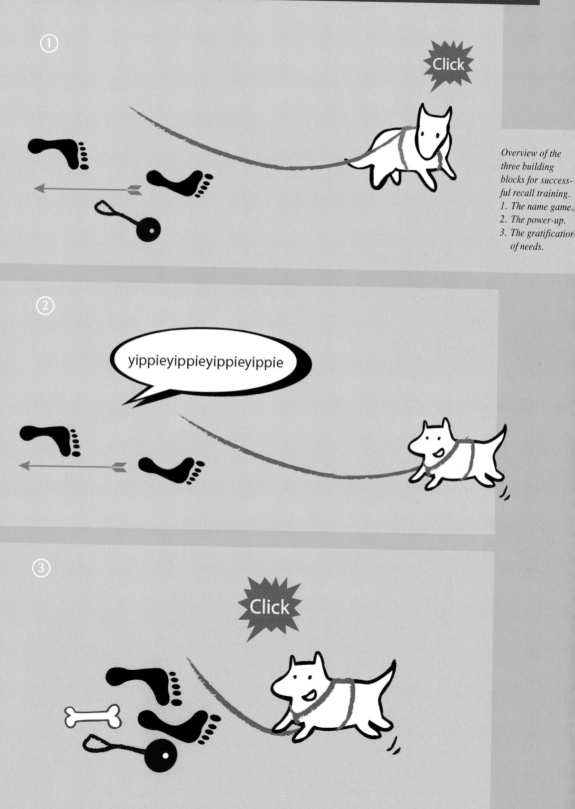

Overview of the three building blocks for successful recall training.
1. The name game.
2. The power-up.
3. The gratification of needs.

Maria has addressed Maya by name; Maya turns around – 'click' – reward.

En route Maya gets her treat thrown towards her as a reward that can be sniffed out.

②

Maya is on her way back to Maria after a successful reorientation. Maria is now walking backwards and is supporting Maya with her power-up signal.

③

Getting to play a tug-of-war game with Maria with a rope made of fleece is a great boon for Maya.

'Click' – Maya is here!

Tip!
You should invest sufficient time to train the absolutely reliable recall – it's definitely worth your while!

If your dog has really understood the recall, you can add in a quiet little exercise after the reward: Sit, down, touch. Afterwards your dog can have some time to do what they like again. Release them with a 'Run!' and a sweeping gesture. Another variation you might use is to put the dog on the leash *after* the reward and to walk with them on the leash for a while.

Important!
When walking on rough terrain, as a rule a dog who has not yet reliably learned the recall ought to be put on a leash or drag line. If you have a good overview, you can of course let them run free. Don't attempt to recall the dog when there is a lot of distraction and you have not yet done sufficient training.

Undesired behaviour – misbehaviour?

When dogs don't 'function' in certain situations as well as the human would like, this is often called undesired behaviour or misbehaviour. Sometimes it is also alleged that the dog is striving to gain power over their human, or even that the dog is trying to ridicule the person. Do you really believe that a dog gives any thought to the possibility of making you the subject of public mockery? Dogs do what they do. They are dogs and they react to their environment. In doing so, they sometimes blot out their human because they have spotted something seemingly more interesting or dangerous. Behaviour is determined by its consequences. If the dog's reactions are always the same in certain situations, that is because they have *learned* this behaviour in these situations. For *them* this way of reacting works.

The work with a clicker/marker tends to be criticised because you can't use it to 'terminate' 'undesired' behaviour. As described in the preceding chapters, behaviour is influenced to a large degree by the consequences that result from it. Consequently, desired behaviour has to be practised in those same situations in which the dog has previously learned to behave in an 'undesired' manner. How are you going to achieve this without using a clicker/marker?

Using conventional methods, you have to wait until the dog displays the 'wrong' reaction in a certain situation, in order to be able to 'correct' them. This means nothing but punishing the dog in order to stop the behaviour, or rather to suppress it. In the chapter that describes the foundations for learning (see page 22 ff.) you learned that in order for punishment to be effective it has to consist of aversive stimuli, and it has to be so severe that the behaviour is never displayed ever again. If you are forced to punish your dog again for similar misbehaviour, the first punishment was not enough for them. The dog had been punished unnecessarily.

In addition we cannot ignore the emotional aspect of the matter. Dogs associate painful stimuli with the things on which they are focusing their attention during the punishment. Are you one hundred percent sure precisely what your dog is taking in as you pull hard on the leash? What actually does your dog learn, if they are always punished when they see another dog? Exactly – coming across other dogs means pain and anger from their human. The other dog becomes a signal for negative emotions that triggers an aggressive reaction, which is appropriate, at least from your dog's point of view. On top of this the dog's aggressive reaction will often be rewarded when the other dog moves away. They have got what they wanted. Aggressive behaviour made the thing that triggered the aggression go away. The dog is not aware of the possibility that the other dog might have walked in the opposite direction anyway. The dog displaying the aggressive reaction has made the following association: Barking means increasing the distance to the object that triggered the

aggression. This turn of events provides relief because the human on the other end of the leash also stops shouting. It is a pleasant emotion that they will receive as the result of the disappearance of the other dog (the trigger). This reinforces the barking and fits of aggression over and over again.

By contrast, with the use of the clicker/marker you have the possibility of modifying undesired behaviour to become a desired reaction associated with positive emotions. To achieve this, it is not even necessary to wait until your dog has done something 'wrong'. You can begin training before this ever happens! Turn the trigger for negative emotions and undesired behaviour into a trigger for positive emotions instead! First of all you have to change your perspective. You know what undesired behaviour looks like. Have you also given some thought to how your dog is supposed to behave 'correctly' in potentially unpleasant moments? You have to think about this as carefully as you would about developing a 'normal' behaviour or an exercise. You know the trigger: a strange dog at a distance of ten metres, for example. Effective learning is not possible while in a state of great excitement. Therefore you have to begin training while your dog is still receptive.

Important!

Your dog has to learn things actively. Only then can they make the right associations. Don't lure the dog, either with treats, or with toys. The strange dog has to become the trigger for the new behaviour – not the treat/toy!

Modifying behaviour – modifying emotions

I won't be able to go into this subject very deeply, because it involves very complex training work. Nevertheless, I would like to explain the principle briefly (see picture page 81).

Step 1: Practising calm behaviour

Practise calm behaviour with your dog when a trigger comes into view (for example another dog) from an acceptable distance. Take your cue from your own dog of what distance that might be. The distances indicated in the picture (page 81) are only examples.

At this point mark and reward every calm behaviour once the other dog has come into view. When you are sure that you can mark any strange dog, and your dog is always calm, proceed to the next step.

Step 2: Reorientation towards the human

Say the dog's name as soon as the trigger appears, in order to draw their attention to you. As soon as your dog turns towards you they should get a click and a reward from you. Again, only advance to the next step once the reorientation is displayed reliably whenever other dogs appear.

Step 3: Calling up an exercise

For this it is of great importance that exercises such as the 'name game' and 'touch' or 'sit' have been learned and generalised really well (see the relevant chapters), and that these have always been structured and called up in a positive manner. We want to modify the emotional associations regarding the

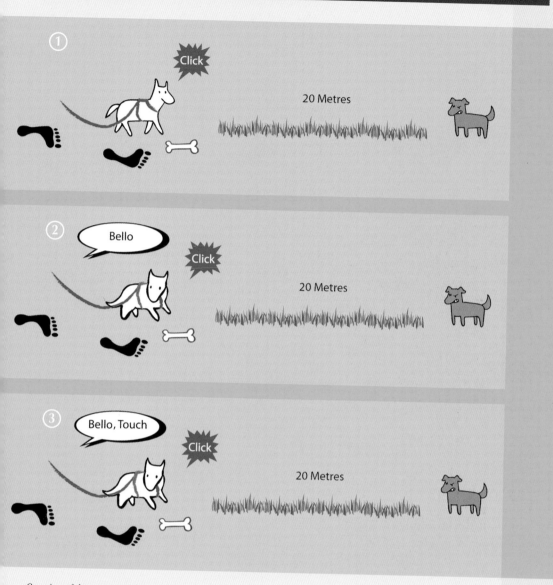

Overview of the separate steps to train 'modification of behaviour'. Calm behaviour (1), reorientation towards the human (2), calling up an exercise (3).

trigger fear/aggression to become positive emotions instead. This will only work if all the components involved are positive: Marker signal, exercise, reward! Every time you modify a behaviour always pay attention to the basic structure of an exercise (see page 80).

You can also use environmental signals as triggers for other exercises. For example, a visitor to the house can serve as a trigger for sitting down. Now you have to become pro-active. Think about exactly what you want your dog to do in this and other situations to enable you to train the desired behaviour carefully.

Luna is looking away from Thomas. He addresses her.

Luna looks towards him – 'click' – reward.

Luna has learned to carry out a little exercise ('Touch') when she sees other dogs.

In this way the other dogs become a signal for turning towards the human's hand.

Because Emma finds large men rather scary, in the past she used to bark at them. Nowadays an 'environmental signal' asks her to turn towards her owner and carry out a calm exercise. Afterwards both can continue their walk in a relaxed manner. Exercises that have been structured in a positive manner are, in effect, small rewards in themselves.

Important!

If you are unsure about how to train more complex behavioural modifications, you should ask a competent dog trainer for help and advice. When choosing a trainer/behavioural consultant you ought to make sure that he or she is familiar with desensitisation and developing alternative behaviour.

A few words in conclusion

Pack leadership, dominance – who is the master of the house?

Pack order problems are often talked about in the dog world in connection with dogs who are difficult to train, usually in order to justify the use of harsh training techniques. The dog owner is supposed to worry about losing their posi-

tion as the 'leader of the pack'. Wild scenarios are set up in order to intimidate the dog or to 'beat' them into submission using techniques that rely on violence. After all, it is said, the canine pack member should have their place at the very bottom of the hierarchy.

Have you ever wondered where these allegations and opinions originated from? They are only opinions, not verifiable facts, and are founded on observations made by behavioural biologists.

Dominance in behavioural biology

The dominance system in behavioural biology is supposed to help humans to recognise social structures. Its purpose is mainly to explain the relationships between individuals. It is therefore an attempt to explain behaviour to enable us to understand it better.

The term 'dominance' was popularised by the Norwegian researcher Schjelderup-Ebbe in the 1920s. He observed the social behaviour of chickens and the relationships between the different individuals. This glimpse inside the chicken coop has given us the strictly linear dominance system that applies to chickens: A pecks B, B pecks C but not A, C pecks D, and so forth. Disastrously, this system was quickly applied to all vertebrates that live in a community. Can it really be right to apply observations that have been made on one species to all other species? Would you like to have your life equated to life in a chicken coop? Probably not.

This model was kept alive in the field of biology until the late 1960s, until observations made on primates in their natural environment showed that it could not be applied to all species. It was observed that there were not just linear hierarchical systems, but a whole range of other relationships among individuals. In this way networks emerge that are characterised by individual relationships, not by constant demonstrations of status and rank.

The next important aspect in the observation of relationships is the context. In which kind of context does an animal 'win' and in what kind of context does it 'lose'? If animal A always 'wins' in the same or similar situations over animal B, A dominates B in these circumstances. But this does not mean that animal A also dominates animal C. It could actually be the other way round. Relationships are varied and not always the same. As soon as animal B manages to dominate animal A once, the relationship has changed. Who is the 'higher ranking' individual in this case?

This type of 'social dominance' is always dependent on the relationships among individuals and on the context. The environment and its conditions always play a major part in the relationship between two animals. We cannot just transfer behaviour to a) a different species and b) a completely different context, while also disregarding the issue of time and location.

Wolves live in a strict hierarchy – or do they really?

In order to make the dominance theory fit, life in a wolf pack is often cited to justify so-called 'rank order reduction plans'. But do these explanations based on decades-old observations still apply? Science is not static. Over time old theories and hypotheses are either confirmed or disproved through new and better documented observations.

The myths, which are unfortunately still circulating today, about the strictly hierarchical wolf pack, which claim that wolves eagerly and frequently fight for higher positions in the pack, were based on observations of wolves living in captivity. In this context wolves who were not related to each other were put in an enclosure together. In this environment their social behaviour was observed. The researchers forgot one thing: Social groups behave differently in captivity from in their natural habitat. Wolves in captivity, who are not related to each other, develop different behaviours. It is true that obvious hierarchical structures emerged. As a result of living in captivity the animals were not able to evade the stressful situation and migrate elsewhere. They had to find other ways of relating to each other and of securing resources, which of course also includes choosing a sexual partner. In captivity the choice of partners is very limited, and this alone will lead to repeated quarrels.

It's like observing human behaviour in a prison camp, and then trying to apply the findings to the rest of humanity. Conditions in a prison camp are obviously rather different from life in freedom. Animals who are kept in fenced-off terrain or in cages have little or no chance to develop and use their natural behavioural repertoire. As a result of the stress many start displaying behavioural abnormalities, abnormalities that would not have emerged in the wild.

What exactly is a wolf pack?

Research conducted in recent decades has shown that the lives of wolves in their natural habitat are different from what had been thought previously. The well-known wolf researcher David Mech has spent almost his entire life observing wolves in their natural habitat.

During fifty years of observing them in the wild he was able to conclude that wolves don't live in strictly linear hierarchical packs, as is often alleged. A wolf pack can be compared to a human family. It consists of one set of parents and their offspring of the last one to three years. The often cited 'alpha couple' does not even feature. We are merely dealing with a social structure, it's quite obvious, that consists of parents and their offspring. All members of the group are related to each other.

In contrast to this are the observations of unrelated wolves in captivity. In addition, the environmental conditions play a very important part in the behaviour of the pack. Not every wolf pack behaves in the same way; much depends on where they live.

However, the most important aspect of Mech's observations is the fact that the offspring leave the wolf family at the onset of sexual maturity, or in response to social pressure, in order find a suitable mate. In this way each wolf has the opportunity to become the founder of a pack. Only very few wolves ever join an existing pack, even if there is any chance of being admitted.

What conclusions can be drawn from these observations, which have been made in the natural environment of the wolf over many years? Wolves don't have a 'power gene' – there are no fights to achieve any kind of hierarchical order, or a virtual notion of 'status'. Wolf packs function like human families: The parents are treated with respect; there may be squabbles among the siblings for this or that resource, and when the time comes, the young adults leave their family group in order to find a partner for sexual reproduction, and in turn start their own family group.

Wolves are very social animals who need closeness and security. Both parents look after their offspring together. The male wolf and the older offspring provide food in order to feed the suckling female wolf, and later the puppies as they grow up. After a successful hunt the puppies are supplied with food by the other pack members. It would make no sense whatsoever to feed the little

ones last, and only give them the leftovers! The female wolf has invested time and energy in the gestation and the suckling of her young; hence they are the first to receive the all important energy source. This ensures that they grow up and reach adulthood.

Dogs are wolves – is this true?

It is popular to cite the wolf–dog comparison when talking about harsh training methods. However, as demonstrated in the previous section the argument regarding rank order does not even hold water in the face of the recent observations of free-living wolves.

Geneticists confirm that the genetic make-up of dogs and wolves is about 99.8 percent identical. But does this justify the transferral of every type of behaviour from wolves to dogs? Let us compare the development and some of the behaviours of dogs and wolves:

- Dogs reach sexual maturity at the age of six months, depending on the breed; wolves are mature only at the age of two years. As a result of domestication, male dogs are able to produce offspring all year round. Female dogs are on heat twice a year; by contrast female wolves come into season only once a year. The existence of a heat period only once a year triggers the reproductive mechanism in the wolf. Consequently, male wolves are not able to reproduce outside this period.

Important!

The differentiating characteristic 'sexual maturity' is associated with some important behaviours in the dog. For example, the constant production of testosterone (male sexual hormone) in the male dog is responsible for aggression towards fellow non-castrated dogs, because these are often in competition. This situation of heightened male competition is even further enhanced in the co-educational group sessions held at many dog training schools.

Another problem inherent in these mixed groups is the fact that, owing to the artificially created training situation, testosterone production is increased even further. A surplus of testosterone precludes relaxed learning and produces stress. The brain can only carry out effective and sustained learning in a stress-free environment. Mixed-group sessions for young dogs up to the age of three years are therefore counterproductive. Often a spiral of pressure and punishment builds up, making the learning process much harder for the dog, or even impossible. Why would we want to make things harder than necessary for an animal that does not have our brain capacity? We humans often find it very hard to take in new information and commit it to long-term memory in stressful situations. Try a self-experiment! Watch your favourite movie while simultaneously trying to learn a poem by heart. The brain isn't able to multitask; it can only truly concentrate on one thing at a time. Distractions always lead to mistakes.

This is what happens to an adolescent male dog who has to attend a mixed training group for his 'basic training'. Always bear in mind that these weekly meetings have nothing to do with the dog's 'normal' home environment – everything dogs learn is associated with a particular context. They have to learn to transfer what they have learned from a low-stimulus meadow to everyday life situations (see chapter on foundations of learning, page 22 ff.)

• The next important difference between wolf and dog is the way they rear their young. Wolves rear their offspring communally in the family. The male wolf contributes by providing food. As far as dogs are concerned only the female is involved with rearing the puppies. The male dog only meets the female during mating, and takes every opportunity to cover other female dogs.

• Grown wolves have a great flight distance and are sceptical or anxious regarding anything new. Even with hand-rearing and good training you cannot turn a wolf into a relaxed family dog. By contrast, our domesticated dogs are able to learn new things and cope with different situations all their lives. The socialisation process (learning from experience) is not concluded forever after the sixteenth week of life; socialisation takes place throughout the dog's life. If this were not the case any behavioural therapy would be impossible, especially for dogs with anxiety problems. However, it may take more time for a mature dog than for a young dog to break learned behavioural patterns, and to channel them into different pathways.

- One particular point that should not be forgotten is the difference in aggressive behaviour. A dog's activities can quickly be blocked by using pressure/punishment. Try that with a wolf! Wolves react to stress/punishment with aggression. This is not a very pleasant situation for a human. A dog who reacts to punishment with aggression because he feels threatened is usually treated inappropriately with more pressure and counter-aggression.

We always have to remind ourselves that we're dealing with a dog here and not with a four-legged human wearing fur! A dog can only ever act and react within the confines of its innate and learned behaviour.

Human interpretations, using phrases such as: 'He is not allowed to growl at you!', only serve to muddy the water and do not relate to the true situation.

Behaviour modification through rank order programmes?

In the previous sections I have tried to explain the emergence and further evolution of the dominance theory, as well as the differences between dogs and wolves. In what way does this knowledge about the differences between the two species help us? First, I would like to address briefly the issue of two different species living together. Does your dog really see you as a fellow member of their species? In my view this is just another typical case of anthropomorphism. We humans don't behave like dogs: We walk on two legs, talk all day and always want to touch everything. These are the characteristics we share with our closest relatives, the chimpanzees – apart from the constant talking.

Because we don't behave like dogs, the assumption that we can form a pack with them is simply incorrect. Dogs are animals who live in a social context. For most of them it is important to have company, and they have been adapted to live and work with humans by a selective breeding process. In biology when two different species live together this is called 'symbiosis'. A symbiosis does not necessarily have to be equally beneficial to both sides.

However, let us assume that we would like to achieve a balanced relationship with our dog. Is this at all possible? Let us have a look at the life of an average family dog. The dog is purchased, and as always there are certain rules that apply to living together in a group. Our family dog gets their food ration divided twice a day, and they are not able to choose what's on the menu. The dog is taken out of the house on a leash at certain intervals in order to do their business. Some dogs are never allowed the pleasure of running free off the leash, or to gratify their need to do so. The dog must not disturb the humans at the table, they are not allowed to bark when the doorbell rings, they are only allowed to sleep in one particular spot in the house, and all day long they are told what to do by the humans. Would you wish for such a life?

The term 'dominance' in behavioural ecology

In the previous chapters the term 'dominance' has been described from the point of view of behavioural biology. But this is not the only discipline where this term is used. Behavioural ecology is a sub-discipline within biology. It describes research into the relationships among organisms and with their environment. In ecology those species that are most prevalent in their habitat are called dominant (they have the greatest biomass). These species determine the structure of a habitat. In other words, they dominate their specific environment. The best example is the human species. We have the greatest biomass – even if there are more ants in this world – and we control our environment to a huge degree. Resources such as food, raw materials and land are exploited by humans, often without any consideration whatsoever. Other species have to react to the fact that their portion of the natural environment that is still untouched by human activity is getting less and less, and they are forced to retreat.

With regard to dominance theory in ecology (see box) we humans are the 'dominant species' from the very start. We control the environment and access to resources. However, these general rules governing our lives together often don't directly affect problem behaviour.

Rank order programmes cannot solve behavioural problems

In my practice of behavioural counselling I often deal with dogs who display fear or aggressive behaviour. However, rank reduction programmes don't provide any help with these front-line problems. They merely help humans to stick to a few rules regarding their lives shared with a dog. This is actually not such a bad thing. But it doesn't help a dog in specific situations in which it reacts with fear or aggressive behaviour. We are dealing with a living creature who displays those particular emotions much more readily than a human being. The reason for this lies in the structure of the brain. Mammals share basically the same brain structure – that's why in many fields of research (medicine, biology) mice, rats or monkeys are used as research subjects. Environmental stimuli are evaluated with respect to their emotional content in the midbrain; in addition, important information is filtered from the unimportant on its way to the cerebrum. This protects the thought centre from being overloaded.

In mammals the part of the cerebrum that evaluates the emotional content of environmental stimuli is proportionally larger, because for reasons of self-preservation dangerous situations have to be recognised quickly. Humans who suffer from arachnophobia, for example, are familiar with this problem. Even though they have never been harmed by a spider, they get scared or have panic attacks at the mere sight of one of these little arachnids, even if the spider knows how to behave itself. With rank order programmes the situation is similar. How will the fact that they have learned always to walk through the door behind their human help a dog in a specific situation?

All environmental stimuli are evaluated with respect to their emotional content; it's the same with all animals. According to this theory, a fear or anxiety problem or exaggerated aggressive behaviour can only be modified in certain situations by modifying the emotions associated with the trigger.

Please bear in mind that dogs learn through association; they associate their behaviour with the consequences in certain situations.

Imagine your dog, who is on a leash, reacting aggressively when they catch sight of another dog because they want to put some more distance between them and this fear-inducing object. At the same time you also react with aggression in response to your dog's aggression, and give the leash a forceful jerk. What association will the dog make regarding the trigger of all this? That the approach of a strange dog indicates pain. By doing this you don't modify the emotional situation associated with the appearance of a strange dog in any desired direction. You often just make matters worse, and a spiral of escalating punishments ensues as a result.

Your dog can only react according to what you have conveyed to them. If you want to influence emotions and behaviour in a positive manner, you have to turn the fear-inducing trigger into one that is a source of happiness, and in addition train alternative behaviours. Instead of waiting until the dog becomes trapped in a cycle of fear, begin slowly to guide them in a positive direction every time they see a strange dog by using 'click and reward' before the event. Positively structured signals such as the use of the dog's name to encourage reorientation (see page 51 ff.) already trigger positive emotions.

If your dog is unable to carry out a well structured and learned signal, then the reason is that their brain isn't playing ball. The centre of emotions just won't allow the signal to penetrate any further towards the thinking part of the brain. If this is the case no amount of strict intervention will resolve the situation. You'll only end up poisoning your positive signal, get sucked into another spiral of punishment, and the dog will once more associate negativity with the trigger. In the chapter about behavioural modification (see page 9 ff.) I have described in detail how you can influence and modify behaviour positively in specific situations. In this way your dog learns with lasting effect how to deal with those difficult moments in life. Work on the specific situations in which your dog displays abnormal behaviour, and don't waste your time and effort with outdated rank reduction programmes.

Thanks again – a second time!

I would like to thank all those people who have helped me with this book, just by being there, or by taking part in discussions, contributing ideas, or offering criticism:

My parents, in whose garden I have entered my thoughts into my laptop, and who have looked after me and spoilt me in 'Hotel Mama'.

My special thanks go to Dr. rer. nat. Ute Blaschke-Berthold, biologist. The depth of her subject knowledge, her untiring efforts regarding new scientific findings in the field of learning behaviour, biology and dog training, and many virtual discussions have enabled me to widen my horizons, something that might not have happened in this way without this exchange. Many thanks to you, dear Ute, for reading my manuscript.

My dear Maria Rehberger of Hundetraining Nürnberg, with her dogs Emma and Maya, who was always there when I needed her as an assistant, model for videos and photos and proofreader. The same goes for Astrid Hintermeier, with Luna, who read my manuscript with great diligence and with the eye of a publisher. Training with Luna has greatly improved my reaction time. And thank you Thomas (and Luna) – men who work with the clicker are unfortunately still very few and far between.

I would also like to thank my clients who have decided to opt for violence-free dog training and working with a marker with me, and who have realised that it does the trick.

A special thanks to those trainers who have influenced me a great deal through their books and/or seminars: Kay Laurence, Patricia McConnell, Jean Donaldson, Birgit Laser, Turid Rugaas, who have been working for years in violence-free ways with humans and their dogs, and in doing so have proved that you can do without pronged collars, orgies of dominance, and the tones of a drill sergeant.

Many thanks to my dogs Usha and Louis, and waiting on the other side of the rainbow bridge are James, Hudson and especially Dino – the furry creatures that have changed my life.

Finally I would like to thank my publisher Cadmos for their good cooperation and for providing me with their support as ever.

About the author

Monika Gutmann started her career as a trainer at a club for dog sports, although she felt that she disagreed with too many training practices there. Through a number of seminars, she gained knowledge of training methods based on animal protection and the wellbeing of dogs. In the course of this, she discovered the use of the clicker/marker signal. In 2004, she started her own dog training school 'modern dogs' in Kaufbeuren, Germany. Since relocating to Weißenburg in 2008, she has been successfully running courses focusing on behavioural advice and therapy. Monika Gutmann is an accredited member of the International Association of Professional Dog Trainers.

Further reading

Bekoff, Mark: *Das Gefühlsleben der Tiere*. Bernau: Animal Learn, 2008

Bradshaw, John W. S./Blackwell, Emily J./Casey, Rachel A.: Dominance in domestic dogs – useful construct or bad habit? Journal of Veterinary Behavior: Clinical Applications and Research 4 (3), 109–144, May/June, 2009

Dennison, Pamela S: *How to Right a Dog Gone Wrong. A Road Map for Rehabilitating Aggressive Dogs*. Crawford: Alpine Blue Ribbon Books, 2005

Hallgren, Anders: *Das Alpha-Syndrom*. Bernau: Animal Learn, 2006

Killion, Jane: *When Pigs fly! Training Success with Impossible Dogs*. Wenatchee: Dogwise Publishing, 2007

Laser, Birgit: *Clickertraining. Das Lehrbuch für eine moderne Hundeausbildung*. Brunsbek: Cadmos, 2000

Laurence, Kay: *Learning about Dogs: Clicker Novice Training*. Level 2. Sunshine Books Inc., 2006

Laurence, Kay: *Learning about Dogs: Clicker Intermediate Training*. Level 3. Selbstverlag, 2003

McConnel, Patricia B.: *Liebst Du mich auch? Die Gefühlswelt bei Mensch und Hund*. 2. Aufl. Nerdlen: Kynos, 2008

McConnel, Patricia B.: *Das andere Ende der Leine. Was unseren Umgang mit Hunden bestimmt*. 9. Aufl. Nerdlen: Kynos, 2008

Mech, David L.: *Was ist eigentlich mit dem Begriff Alpha-Wolf passiert?* Artikel zum Download im PDF-Format. www.cumcane.de, 2008

Miller, Pat: *The Power of Positive Dog Training*. Howell Book House, 2001

Panksepp, Jaak: *Affective Neuroscience: The Foundations of Human and Animal Emotions* (Series in Affective Science). Oxford: Oxford University Press, 2004

Parsons, Emma: *Click to Calm: Healing the Aggressive Dog*. Sunshine Books Inc., 2004

Pryor, Karen: *Reaching the Animal Mind: Clicker Training and What It Teaches Us About All Animals*. Scribner Book Inc., 2009

Pryor, Karen: *Don't Shoot the Dog!: The New Art of Teaching and Training*. 3rd Revised edition. Lydney: Ringpress Books Ltd., 2002

Wilhelm, Klaus: *Oxytozin – Elixier der Nähe*. Gehirn und Geist 1/2, 2009

Zimbardo, Philip G.: *Psychologie*. Berlin, Heidelberg: Springer, 1992

Index

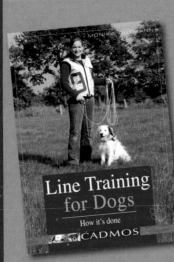